transformed

AND transparent

Transformed and Transparent

© 2007 by Tandra Johnson

ISBN 978-0-6151-6312-3

Unless otherwise marked, Scripture quotations are taken from The Holy Bible, New International Version (NIV) ©1973, 1984 by International Bible Society. Also quoted, The Holy Bible, New King James Version (KJV)

Definitions are taken from The American Heritage® Dictionary of the English Language, Fourth Edition. Copyright © 2006 by Houghton Mifflin Company. Published by Houghton Mifflin Company. All rights reserved.

Printed in the United States of America

Design & Publishing by

Tandra Johnson

PO Box 996

Allen, Texas 75013

www.tandrajohnson.com

DEDICATION

To God Be the Glory!

I am forever indebted to my dad and Barbara for being my lifelines.

My daughter, Krissandra, I praise God he gave me you. Thank you for giving me the desire to live.

These words would still be hidden in the pages of my journal had it not been for the wise counsel of a dear friend, Rev. Marcus King. Thank you for being the conduit in helping me to look beyond what I see.

INTRODUCTION

I am living with two incurable diseases. For more than two years of my life I have had to listen to doctors tell me that I'm "Treatable, Not Curable". I know what it is like to go to sleep and not want to wake up. I know what it is like to smile on the outside and have no one discern that you are dying on the inside. I am what my senior pastor, Dr. Frederick D. Haynes, III calls a "wounded winner", and I wear my scars with honor.

For almost 60 days during the summer of 2005, I could not hide or dress up my sickness. My issue of Pustular Psoriasis, a chronic skin disorder, was no longer private. The door was closed to pride. There was no room for vanity. I have gone through hell in private, and now it is time to come out in public.

People look at me now and do not know what I have been through. For weeks the doctors could not diagnose the problem. From my scalp to the soles of my feet, my skin went through a painful metamorphosis. My body was covered with pustules, my skin was sticky and stinky, and the layers of both my hands and feet completely peeled off.

The media is saturated with beautiful people that have not gone through anything who tell people how to love themselves. It is time for people, like me, who have felt they were never good enough and not pretty enough to show that love and acceptance starts within; that it takes the one, true, living God to do an extreme makeover from the inside out. I can now say with confidence, "I am beautiful," but I had to go through an ugly process.

Doctors and psychiatrists make millions of dollars each year guiding people through a process of healing. But it takes going through something traumatic and life changing to realize that it takes more than books and 10 steps to not only be healed but to be made whole. Physically I still live with both of these diseases. However, spiritually, mentally, and emotionally, I am healed. I am liberated. I know who I am in Christ Jesus, and I not only love myself, I like myself. As I continue to walk by faith, I know that physical healing will manifest so that God will get His glory.

I have always journaled but little did I know at the time that I was documenting a message that would edify and encourage. God made me over. I now have a platform to raise awareness about the importance of trusting Him through life's adversities. I hope my story will challenge people to acknowledge their hurts, to love and accept themselves unconditionally, and I want this to speak life into the person who is depressed and discouraged.

- CONTENTS-

Transformation Proclamation

I, _____ hereby proclaim:

I will love and accept myself NOW! I will choose joy no matter what my circumstances. I will not give up, and I will no longer put myself down. I am not a victim. I am a victor. My past does not dictate who I am. Each day when I look in the mirror, I will say at least one positive thing about myself. I will walk in certainty, confidence, and by faith.

Signed _____ Date _____

tes.ti.mo.ny\n.

An assertion offering firsthand authentication of a fact

A public declaration regarding a religious experience

Do You See What I See?

July 3, 2005

The past few days have been turmoil, pain, confusion, and a time that I have been close to the edge. My body, from my scalp to my legs had a severe flare up. I look grotesque, and I am really scared of permanent damage. Is this is a test of my identity and my character. Do I know who I am? Do I still think I am beautiful no matter what the external looks like? Yes and Yes. God is setting me up. He is testing me in every doctor's mess up. He is testing me each time I look in the mirror when I can barely recognize myself. He is testing me to see if I still trust Him when like Job He lifts the hedge of protection. It has been hard to pray, because I do not know what to say. I just praise. I just remember what He has brought me through. It is too easy for me to go back and hide out in the cave and give up on what He has for me. I refuse to quit. I will be blessed exceedingly and abundantly. I will give God the glory, because I will not stop telling this story. My prayer in all this is that I draw closer to Him, that He shows me who I am and what I can do, and that He takes me to a new level in ministry full-time.

July 5, 2005

When Dr. Parker admitted that she did not know what this skin disease is, it blew my mind. When she sent me to the dermatologist for another skin biopsy, I knew that only you God could get me through this. Today has been one of the lowest days I have had since this ordeal with my skin. I know I had to sleep, but it would have been okay with me if I did not wake up. I hurt that bad. I feel so alone and discouraged and angry. Why can't I just be used in a normal way? Why does my brokenness require me to go through all of this? But, God, as I think about my future and my daughter and the thought of sharing my life with someone who will love me unconditionally, all I can say is forgive me. I do believe, but help me with my unbelief. I am strong, but this is a heavy burden to bear. Please show me that I am stronger than I think I am. I am on an emotional roller coaster and minute-by-minute I am up and down. I can be real and honest now. Shoot. You are God. You know how I feel anyway. I may as well be honest. Show me who I am. Tell me what I can do through you. Teach me to look in the mirror as grotesque as I look right now and know that I am beautiful. From the inside out, transform my mind, my heart, my tongue, my ears, and my spine, Father. You are the Potter. Mold, shape, & develop, this clay into your masterpiece.

July 8, 2005

Lord, why did you wake me up?

July 17, 2005

The last 12 days have been a literal hell. The doctors keep running tests, because they do not know what is up or how to treat this. Krissandra is having nightmares about me dying. I am in intense pain physically and emotionally, and whenever I think I am getting better I get worse. I am not hearing God about all this, and it is difficult for me to talk to him right now. I want my body back. I want normalcy. I want to see the sunshine. I want to be serving and surrounded by people at church. I am tired of hiding out in this room because I am too gross to look at. I want this swelling to go down so I can walk again. God give me the strength to endure all of this physically and emotionally. I am all cried out, and I need you NOW. I know you are my healer. I know I am healed. I know that this is a part of the plans you have for me, and I am the witness to your glory and faithfulness, but God I am hurting…trusting but hurting. I do not want Krissandra to continue to see me like this. Burdens are being placed on her that I am feeling guilty about. She has seen me through all this, and in the midst of my tears, I hope she sees my faith, and the hope I have in you. I want this to bring my family closer to you, into your family. Lord, if you are setting me up for ministry, give me vision. Speak Lord clearly and with clarity. The devil is trying to kill me, and I am about to show him that he is a liar. His attack on the 8th did not work. I am more than a conqueror, and I will not be defeated. I will live and not die. I know this is hard on the family to see me this way. And yes, I am suffering, but God I know this is a setup…

July 19, 2005

I walked today! The swelling has finally gone down to the point that I am mobile. And you know what, Rev. King came to visit today. I finally opened up and invited him over to visit. I cannot keep closing him out, and making the call helped me see how much I have grown and how my pride has been cut. Seeing him put a Kool-Aid grin on my face. Even though I did not want him to see me this way, his response to me made me feel like the queen I am forever and a day. Hearing him say I was beautiful, when I know I look like a nightmare and just being with him took me to another place that I did not want to come back from. This wonderful, caring, compassionate man moved beyond himself and really showed me what it is like to be here – physically, emotionally, and spiritually. He spoke to me not where I am but took me into the future. He was real and told me to continue journaling and laying out how I can help educate others on healing. He helped me put a lot in perspective. He made me laugh, and yes I cried (a little).

July 20, 2005

After sitting in Dr. Parker's office and hearing from the dermatologist that they cannot treat this, I got really discouraged. My skin is metamorphosing everyday for the worst, and I am tired of being sick and tired. They got me into UT Southwestern Medical Center, which I am told is the best of the best. While my Great Physician is leading me to healing I am going to trust the hands of the other physicians he is putting me in. The nurse called me back and said they do not accept Cigna HMO, so I will have to pay out-of-pocket. I will do that for some relief. I need it now. God, I need you now.

July 21, 2005

Seven days. That is how long the doctors at UT say it should take for my skin to clear and have relief in sight. I was expecting something different today like a new medical treatment or prognosis. They told me I was a "tough case but a treatable case." Their answer is to double the Prednisone dosage, which will be 40mg. It is like a double-edged sword. I know what the horrible effects are, but I am so desperate for relief. I want to cleanse my body naturally and take the holistic approach as well, but for such a time as this I have got to get some relief. Since I know seven is the number of completion, and it is also the last day of God's test to complete some things He has started in me, it is no coincidence. Manifestation is about to happen…Healing, Wholeness, Love, Prosperity, and Destiny…I am ready to give birth. These labor pains have been intense, and I almost aborted the promise, but thank God for his grace. Today I also had an in-person meeting with Stephanie. Slowly I am allowing people to see me. I am still T. I am over this flesh now. God has got so much more in me that I will not trip on what I know is healed. I claim that and receive that in Jesus name.

July 26, 2005

I have been meaning to write for the last couple days but could not find the motivation. Each time I start to, I look at my skin, and just start peeling it.

July 27, 2005

BELIEVE – I have got to stand firm on God's word and know that I am not only healed, but I am made whole. Yesterday I read about the different people Jesus healed and the way he healed them. He spoke the word. He touched. He felt power leave him when the woman with the issue of blood touched him. I do not know how my healing will manifest, but I know it will. I guess I am expecting some traditional, religious way for it to happen, but I know God has got something bigger planned. After all this, shoot I am expecting him to. It has been real hard to be motivated the past few days. If I had a diaper I would just use the bathroom and lay in bed wishing away the pain, the peeling, the awful smell of skin and ultimately what is the breakdown and teardown of my skin. Once I make the first move to get up, I am okay but it takes hours to want to move. I continue to tell God I love him. I beg for help. I plead for him to have mercy and hear my cry, yet I am still like this. If I had known I would have to go through this to get to my destiny I can guarantee you that I would have missed out. But somehow God knew what I could endure. He knew I would throw a few Tandra Tantrums. He knew I would have moments of misery. He even knew there would be days that I would not talk to him, and I would play the quiet game. I was real good at it for a couple days, too. Then I began to think about life and why I am here. I do not want to be in this place looking at my body this way. I want my Mac to be tight. I want clear, flawless skin. But I do not have that now. You know what I have learned in all this is that beauty is truly skin deep. Before any skin flare-up with psoriasis, I was Tandra Johnson – beautiful, smart, charismatic, passionate, helpful, organized, loving, caring, yeah all that and then some. You know what, even now with my skin disfigured and my still being a little vain about all this, I am still all that and then some. I have asked God to help me to deal with any insecurity and jealousy I am still harboring. I do not want to compare myself to anyone else.

I may not have long hair, be bright and thick with luscious lips, but I am beautiful. Since I have to go through all this, I have got to reflect and process. I have got to ask questions. I have got to learn something and be able to educate and help someone else.

I am up writing tonight, because I do not want to sleep. I have been excessively sweating because of the Prednizone, and it makes my skin sticky and it stinks. Nights are miserable so I figured I would make the most of this one and use my time wisely instead of staring into space and having a pity party. This is about to be over. When it is I want to be able to give a message of hope to everyone who is down and wants to stay down and to everyone who is up right now on how to manage and maintain when the low days come. There is too much life to live and help to give, and I am willing to do what God would have me to in order for this not to be in vain. God, please help me to communicate this in your words, help others with your love, and minister through my private pain.

Talk To Me
A Personal Interview

Q:
Who is this affecting?

Krissandra – She is having bad dreams. I do not know the long-term effect this will have on her. She has seen me through all this – the shakes & helping me shower and walk when I could not, seeing me cry and get mad, but also seeing me praise and endure through all this. I know she has been scared right along with me, but she does not show it or tell me. I have got to have her talk to someone about her feelings and handle this the right way. The Single Parent Conference theme epitomizes Krissandra, "Thanks for My Child!" I have needed her and from getting my pills, rubbing me down, encouraging me not to give up, to staying up until 6am in the morning having pickle conversations, she has been at my beckon call. She has missed going some places and doing some things because of me. I will make it up to her.

Dad & Barbara – Being here is a blessing all by itself. Emotionally, I know they are stressed and worried. They are doing a lot to take care of me: picking up medicine, checking up on me, making sure I get to the doctor, getting me and Krissandra whatever we need, and I am appreciative of that. I know Dad does not like seeing me this way, no one does, but it is harder on him. To lose a wife and daughter and now have to see his baby girl go through all this has to be hell. I can see the pain on his face and all the emotional stress. I know he is talking to you God. Answer him and tell him that I am breaking this curse. I am healed and restored and because of me he will come back to you. I prayed with Barbara, because she has been phenomenal in checking up on me and going out of her way to help me. I pray that I be the example of faith and hope that will bring her to accepting Jesus as Lord. Do not let me take their love for granted. Do not let me forget to say, "Thank You" and celebrate all the sacrifices they are making for me.

Dre –He walked in on me crying one day, and I know that had a negative effect on him. He does not deal with things anyway, so Father let him not hold his feelings in. I do not want him to drink more because of me and this situation. If I could talk to him more, I think he will be okay. Yeah, I will make him talk, and I will keep him updated. He is picking up Deon today, so I hope he will fill him in on everything that has been going on before they make it here. I know he will.

Family - Of all the family (outside of my immediate), Alicen has been the only one showing up to help, to give me information, to buy the natural stuff for my skin…just an awesome caregiver. I have not received any other calls or personal visits just to see me. Today I jokingly told her to let everyone else know that I am not contagious, but I was real serious.

Friends – I have not told everyone, but thank you God for Rev. King, Esterlyn, CC, Stephanie, Tina and Diane for their visits and calls and all their encouragement and prayers. I am grateful that they are surrounding me with love.

Q: What have been my emotions and feelings?

A: Anger.

Frustration. Insecurity.

Loneliness. Questioning. Hopelessness.

Depression. Loneliness. Discouraged.

Encouraged. Miserable. Ready to give up. Motivated. Afraid.

Q: What would I tell someone who is about to give up?

A: Praise can save your life. At my lowest points, even when I was not feeling God, I would tell him that I loved him. I would just say, "Thank you for my life." Sometimes I would just say, "Have Mercy." My prayer daily was "For every step I take you take 10, and then when I cannot go any further, carry me." He has definitely done that, and I thank him. Even when I did not think He was near, He was there, and He brought me through at my specific point of need.

More Than Words

Q: When this is over, what do you want people to know?

1.
Don't be afraid of death; be afraid of the unlived life.

The devil should have killed me when he had the chance. Since I am still alive, there must be something God wants me to do. I do not know when I will experience that last heartbeat, and there is so much life that I want to live. I still have not taken my safari. I want to ride a motorcycle. One day I want to fly First Class. I will walk down the aisle one day and say, "I Do". I need to teach Krissandra how to put on makeup, and I want to be there when she experiences her first date and prom and graduation. There are so many desires I have not fulfilled. What if I dare to dream? What if I look beyond these circumstances and LIVE? I have to feel like I'm doing the opposite of what Satan expects. Life is better than what I have been living, and my future is waiting on me. It is time for me to get out of this waiting room and resuscitate the desires of my heart.

2.

Don't run from suffering.

There are valuable lessons in life that cannot be learned by any other means. Years ago I heard a quote that has always been embedded in my spirit, "The struggle is a part of how the butterfly emerges." I can so relate to this, because I know that once upon a time I was that slimy little worm hiding out in the cocoon of life. It was a lonely place, but in that darkroom is where God developed the negative in my life. I am learning that God wants to take those places that are bruised and hurt and fill it with His love. Why did it take me so long to realize this? Jesus is not oblivious to my pain, my hurt, or to my needs. He also knows just how long, how much, how deeply I have been hurting, too. Now that I have learned not to suppress my feelings, God has definitely shown me some stuff through my tears. I have given myself permission to hurt and even though it is rough, I am going to endure. I have got to go through this to get to everything he has for me.

3.

When you can't pray, Praise.

Even though my heart is broken and my body is fragmented, I will not allow my spirit to be broken. My issues will not keep me from giving God praise. I will initiate my own blessing. Psalm 34:1 says, "I will bless the Lord at all times. His praise shall continually be in my mouth." In spite of my situation, I choose to praise the Lord. I choose to give thanks. I choose to clothe myself in a garment of praise for my spirit of heaviness. I am going to continue to put on these CDs and just listen to the words. And when I do not know what to say, I will just repeat them over and over. I will let them marinate in my spirit so I can taste the flavor of God's goodness. My faith is the doorway He is going to use to activate all this potential that He placed within me. I am not giving up before my breakthrough.

4.

Be real with your feelings, especially if it hurts like hell.

As hard as this is, I am giving myself permission to hurt. A lot of us Christians fail to do what Jesus did with the lame man by the Pool of Bethesda. We fail to acknowledge the reality of people's hurts. We avoid the subject, because it makes us uncomfortable, or we tell people, "You are not supposed to hurt. If you were a real Christian, if you were truly spiritual, you would not feel this way." That is a lie and the truth ain't nowhere in that. I am tired of people hiding behind their spiritual masks and making you feel guilty for having a "down day". If you hurt, be real with God and tell him how you really feel. It is not like He is going to be surprised.

5.

Ask God what you should learn, even if you don't understand what He is doing.

I love the story of Job, because he rested in what he did not understand. Problems will not go away. Rejection will not go away. Hurt will not go away. But God gives us confidence as to what He is doing in our lives. Even when friends judge and reject you, do not answer your critics. Everyone will have an opinion as to what you are going through and why...do not even bother. Do not listen to your body. Do not listen to doubt and fear. Listen to Jesus. Listen to His Word! Be concerned with what you can do WITH God and not what you can get FROM God.

6.

Look for ways to turn your misery into a message of hope.

I am so grateful for the advice Rev. King gave me to take the focus off of me and to pray for and encourage someone else. There are so many females that I know I could bless through my story. We can be so vain when it comes to our flaws and imperfections. If they could see me looking like this, I am confident that "beauty is only skin deep" would no longer be a cliché. I want to minister to those who are struggling with acceptance and low self-esteem. Help me to connect with all the people who feel they are not pretty enough. My hope is to one day be able to take all of this and use it to speak life into that person who is in despair & discouragement, who feels rejected, who looks in the mirror everyday wishing they were someone else. I know that how I go through this has a lot to do with how I come out. I am not going to just talk a good talk; I am going to walk a good walk and be the right kind of example. The Lord wants me to give glory to Him for what He has done, and this will also serve to help build faith in someone else.

7.

Don't isolate yourself.

Sometimes you may feel like you are the only one "going through", and no one else understands your pain. Let me tell you, there are millions of hurting people, people who do not have it all together, people with scars, people with wounds so deep and some so incredibly sore that it just takes a word or a look to open the scab and create fresh hurt on top of hurt. Trouble will show you who is with you. If the phone does not ring or the cards and visits do not come, you have got to encourage yourself. There are a lot of folks saying I am down for the count. Some people have already written me off. BUT, I am about to let them know that they cannot eulogize me. My life is just beginning.

8.

Have the right attitude while you wait.

Our attitude determines how far we go in reaching our dreams. Too often we accept the limits of a chicken coop and do not even know about the mountains and the winds. We wind up hopping and pecking through life instead of soaring like eagles. I want to fly high. I believe I can fly. Life may let you down, but God lifts us up. Choose to have a good day. No more excuses. The pity party has been cancelled. Separate yourself from negative people and situations. Go to a new place in life, love, and liberty.

9.

<u>Get your finances in order.</u>

In short, handle your business, even before something traumatic happens. I can relate to the woman with the issue of blood who spent everything she had trying to find a cure, who was desperate to get some relief. Having insurance, but not having it accepted has been taxing on my pocketbook. I will not complain, though, because I have been blessed to be able to pay the expenses, get my medication, and still have money in the bank. I now know how important it is to have a savings account and other resources. It is enough to have your issues. It is a whole other level of stress to have to deal with financial burdens on top of your issues.

Q: **What has been the recurring message you have been hearing through all this?**

A: **Praise!!!**

Being thankful...anyhow and anyway. No matter how bad it gets, I am going to make it through this. My praise is more than spiritual ecstasy. I have got a love jones for God.

School Of Hard Knocks

Q:
: What have you learned about yourself in all this?

1.

This is not about my flesh. It is about what God put in me. I can look beyond what people say and know that I am being changed from the inside out.

2.

I am stronger than I thought, and I am willing to fight for what I want. The more the devil puts on me, the more dangerous I am becoming.

3.

It is okay to give myself permission to hurt and to express my emotions. I am human and suppressing my feelings is more detrimental to my health.

4.

To love myself unconditionally, and I know that I am beautiful from the inside out. It is only because he showed me the ugliness before he started beautifying me.

5.

Pain is a lonely journey, and I cannot get upset because no one wants to ride with me. Even though the people I expected to call did not, the people who did were unexpected blessings of encouragement.

"Thank you God for speaking to me as I am up on this night. I will tell my story so you will get your glory."

There Is Hope

July 28, 2005

"Doesn't her mom look scary?" That is what I heard little Ajani say as I walked through the house to my room today. While that was painful to hear, that is my reality. I went to the doctor today, and they were baffled that their prescription did not work on the double dosage. Now they are bringing in the "big guns" to treat this. I am desperate to have this suppressed. I know there is healing, but right now I want to see my body without flakes and lesions and redness. Today I was expecting something miraculous to happen. I am determined. I am desperate. All I want is to lead a fruitful, productive life with the people I love and who love me. I want to minister to all the hurting people who do not know that God will heal them everywhere they hurt. I need vision. I need direction. I need provision. I need strength, because I know I will have my weak moments. This day symbolizes the number of completion. God, what have you finished in me? What can I expect to wake up to on the day of new beginnings? Whatever it is, thank you.

July 31, 2005

Ever since I started the Cyclosporine on Thursday my skin is starting to clear, and I look a whole lot better. I thought having this happen would change the way I felt, but right now I still want the healing to manifest. I do not just want to treat this, although I am grateful for the relief. Esterlyn came and picked me up, and we hung out at her new place today. She has truly been a blessing during this…letting me vent and be real, encouraging me and being like a sister to me. She has been a lifeline through all this. I am not giving up, and although I may still have an occasional low, I am staying up so that I can receive all that He has for me. I am determined for you, God.

August 4, 2005

I felt like a celebrity today at the doctor's office. They were impressed with the way the new medication is working, and they are decreasing the Prednisone gradually. Please let this work, Lord. I am so grateful for the fact that my skin is clearing. I am feeling better, and I am ready to do what I am purposed to do. Today was the first day in about three weeks that I have been able to take a shower. That is a big deal, because I have been taking wipe offs because of my skin being so raw. Tonight was a celebration of Curtine's birthday. I got sent a plate. No one has been to visit. They just send a "Hello" with Krissandra or my Dad and Barbara. That is what hurts...especially from my Christian family members. Oh, well, so much for the love. I am over it. It is helping me to get through anyway, because in the future I may, too, not receive the love from those I expect. Help me Lord, to love and support and encourage them in spite of them.

August 5, 2005

Today is the first day of Single Parent-Kid Weekend and a hard day for me. The vision is fruition. Thank you God for giving it to me. I may not ever know why I was not able to be there. You gave me the strength to plan and organize and pray to ensure that we had a Five Star conference weekend. I was blessed with a wealth of volunteers and leaders and support, so your provision was made manifest. There is a part of me that wanted to throw on my Mac and try and go. The other part of me knew that I needed to have my butt right here at home. It is hard to put my feelings into words right now. All I know is lives will be changed, and that is what is important. I am learning to look beyond me and realize that God is truly using me for His glory. I am so ready to be an example of hope and mercy and His unfailing love. God, please give me a strategy for sharing my story. This is all about you.

August 6, 2005

I feel so good about myself right now, because I took Krissandra shopping, even with my skin not being completely cleared. I do not care if people stare or question what is wrong with me in their minds. It is not that bad now, and even if it was, I have got to live. I am tired of hiding out inside this room. This is just flesh. I know I am beautiful. I know I need to let Krissandra see me back in stride again. I do not want her worrying about me anymore. This has been hard on her, even if she does not admit it to me. We will talk about how all this has been for her, though. I am getting past being self-conscious, and everyday God is clearing me up and making me more and more beautiful from the inside out.

August 8, 2005

A month ago today I did not want to live, but today as I celebrated my birthday I realized that I have so much to live for. This whole experience has taught me not to discount what I have been through and to know that people are going through worse things than this and are using their stories to make a difference. That is where I am at now. What do I do, Lord? How do I do this? When do I do this? I need you to lay this out every step of the way. Oh, I will tell it. I will shout it out. You healed me! You delivered me! You showed me who I am in you! Now use me. I did not go through all this for nothing. As I celebrate, I thank you for this day and my life…my family and friends. Thank you for teaching me how to overcome and not give up. This is just the beginning of a new book with Best Seller written all over it.

August 9, 2005

I am still excited today because of the GREAT time I had on my birthday. Having Tina, Shawna, Esterlyn, CC, Stephanie, family and Rev. King over brought sunshine during the night. I have learned to be more appreciative of what people do for me. It always takes going through something to change your perspective, and even though this is not how I would have chosen to do it, I thank God that it is more than words for me now. I have to remember where I was, celebrate where I am, and with great expectancy move towards my future. I trust God enough to lead me every step of the way. He is in the forefront in every area of my life. I am tired of getting in His way.

August 10, 2005

I have got to let go of former things for God to give me a new name, a new identity.

August 11, 2005

I am not going to lay down what I do. I have got to pursue what I love.

August 12, 2005

Today I went out...Yeah!!! I was so excited. I put on a really nice poncho and slacks, put makeup on, and worked the braids I got yesterday. I went to Whole Foods and Ulta to get some natural makeup. I then went and picked up flowers to put on Mom, Shelby, and Renata's grave. Yesterday was mom's birthday. When I drove into the cemetery it really made me appreciative of life, even if it is not going the way I think it should. My devotional was Thirsty Thursdays entitled, "Why Worry", dealing with Matthew 7:31-34 and how we should live each day to its fullest. Knowing that I, too, could be six feet under made me stop and say, "Thank you, God!" I have got too much to live for. I will live and not die. I will not let these imperfections keep me from doing all God has purposed for me. I will not let go until He blesses me with every promise, marriage, ministry, and a financial harvest. I am determined to get it all. He can trust me. I know I have been changed. I am seeking Him for guidance on when and to give me a strategy on how to tell this story so He can get His glory.

August 13, 2005

God was speaking all day today through the spoken Word and written Word. My morning devotional dealt with being chosen and God having a specific purpose for us. Late tonight Bishop Eddie Long preached a sermon that was full of so many nuggets that I needed to hear. Thank you Lord for continuing to speak and letting me know what to do. I am ready to put the pieces of this picture together and share the masterpiece of what you have done in my life. "If they only knew what I have come through. I am a bad somebody." People cannot hate on this glory until they know my story. Worldwide, Father, please help me share it.

August 14, 2005

Rev. Stephens preached a sermon entitled, "Whose report will you believe? They said or God said." God, I am walking by faith and not fact. You have brought me through. You are the ONE! I am out of your way, and I am going to possess the promise. You have given me a vision. You have made promises and plans. I do not need to hear from anyone else. They may have counted me out, but you counted me in. I take you at your Word.

August 24, 2005

Today I found the journal about my journey of healing from mom's death. I wrote all that seven years ago, so it is amazing how God orchestrated all this. I, through God's grace, have come so far. There has been purpose in my pain. Father, please tell me how to put this all together. Do something bigger than me. Do a new thing. Give me Godly wisdom for every decision I make. Increase your anointing so that I can do supernatural things in your name. I already know it is done. Thank you for that!

jour.nal\ n.

a daily record, as of occurrences, experiences, or observations

Documenting how I felt, both good and bad, was the remedy I needed to help me get through this traumatic experience. It has shown me the importance of openly expressing what is on my mind and to not suppress my feelings. Although I have the pictures and a few scars from what I went through, I could have easily forgotten some meaningful insights and very important lessons!

No matter what you are going through, you will need reminders of God's goodness when you get to the place that He would have you to be. The reminders will keep you humble and grateful. I have included a few important tips that I think will be beneficial in helping you get started.

Write About It!

HOW TO JOURNAL

Your journal is your private place to express all your inner thoughts and feelings. It helps you begin to understand yourself and to process your hopes, your fears, and your breakthroughs. You do not have to be a good writer, and no one can write your story for you.

WHAT DO I NEED TO START MY SPIRITUAL JOURNAL?

All you need is a way to record: a notebook or diary and pen, a computer and keyboard, and most importantly, time.

WHAT SHOULD BE INCLUDED?

You can include: bible verses, sermon notes, prayers you have prayed, God's answers to your prayers, personal struggles, how you feel about events, people, situations, and relationships, quotes or phrases, what you learned, whatever is in your heart. Dialogue with yourself.

HOW OFTEN SHOULD I WRITE?

There is no specific frequency. You can write every day, once a week, or less often. For most people, it is good to write at least once a week, if not daily. Always date your entries.

Remember, there is no wrong way to keep a journal. If it works for you, it is right. You have got a lot to gain, and nothing to lose, by documenting your life and discovering yourself. Start Today!

Do you believe that God loves you and can use you no matter what you or others think about you? The Bible says that you are "fearfully and wonderfully made"---specially created by a loving Father to be a unique person with your own strengths and abilities. The God who knew you before you left your mother's womb has a special purpose in mind for you (Psalm 139:13-14).

Satan would have us believe that there is no way out. He wants us to feel that we are not good enough, smart enough, or pretty enough. If you have ever been sick, discouraged, depressed or felt hopeless, I have provided some scriptures and a relevant devotional that will strengthen your body, mind, and spirit. Whatever you are going through, whatever you are feeling, please know

"IT IS TIME TO H.E.A.L."

HOLLA

It hurts! It is good to make a joyful noise, but sometimes you have just got to make some noise.

EXHALE

Blow out the anxiety, the worry, disappointment, and unforgiveness. When you squeeze a tube of toothpaste, you get toothpaste. What needs to ooze out of you?

ACCEPT

Sometimes pain is like a tough piece of meat. No matter how long you chew on it, you eventually have to swallow it. It may be rough going down, but you will eventually digest it.

LET GO!

God can mend your broken heart, but you must give him all the pieces. Lot's wife was given a second chance, but she couldn't let go of her past and consequently forfeited her future.

med·i·ta·tion\ n.

A devotional exercise of or leading to contemplation

WHAT TO DO WHEN YOU FEEL DISCOURAGED

John 14:1

"Do not let your hearts be troubled. Trust in God; trust also in me.

John 14:27

Peace I leave with you; my peace I give you. I do not give to you as the world gives. Do not let your hearts be troubled and do not be afraid.

2Corinthians 4:8-9

We are hard pressed on every side, but not crushed; perplexed, but not in despair; 9persecuted, but not abandoned; struck down, but not destroyed.

Be Encouraged

◆ ◆ ◆ ◆ ◆ ◆ ◆ ◆ ◆ ◆ ◆ ◆ ◆ ◆ ◆ ◆

"Anxiety in a man's heart weighs it down, but an encouraging word makes it glad." Proverbs 12:25

Have you ever had a day where nothing seemed to go right? Is there a person or a situation you are worrying about? Maybe you are unemployed and help from your friends and family ran out just as quickly as your money did. Or maybe you are feeling down because you have been disappointed, disgraced, or diseased. The Most High God is in control of every situation, every circumstance, so do not let the worries or concerns of the day get you down. This scripture inspires me to give myself a pep talk and remind God of every promise He has made in His word. Begin today to do the same. "God, you are not a man that you should lie. You said you would keep me in perfect peace, because my mind is stayed on you. I am weak right now, so I know your strength will be made perfect. Your grace is sufficient. I know that none of the weapons formed against me shall prosper. There are so many uncertainties in my life right now, so I am acknowledging you, because I know you will direct my path." Speak the Word into your worries, your bank account, your discouragement, and your despair. He is your burden-bearer and heavy-load-sharer. It feels good to hear an encouraging word from others, but reach deep down inside and ask God to strengthen you in your inner man so that you can encourage yourself.

Prayer: Father, please help me to understand what you are doing through the trials and tests in my life. When I face adversity or disappointments, show me how to count it all joy and trust that you are showing me how the truth of your Word makes me glad. I want to trust you. This I ask in the name of Jesus, Amen.

WHAT TO DO WHEN YOU ARE IN NEED OF COURAGE

Psalm 27:14

Wait for the Lord; be strong and take heart and wait for the Lord.

1 Peter 4:12-13 KJV

Dear friends, do not be surprised at the painful trial you are suffering, as though something strange were happening to you. 13But rejoice that you participate in the sufferings of Christ, so that you may be overjoyed when his glory is revealed.

Psalm 31:24 KJV

Be of good courage, and he shall strengthen your heart, all ye that hope in the Lord.

Live Free Or Die Hard

◆ ◆ ◆ ◆ ◆ ◆ ◆ ◆ ◆ ◆ ◆ ◆ ◆ ◆ ◆ ◆

1 Samuel 16:1a - Now the Lord said to Samuel, "You have mourned long enough."

Before I jumped more than 13,000 feet, my skydive instructor told me, "The hardest part is letting go!" While reading today I was reminded of that experience and could relate to what Samuel was going through. He had anointed Saul to be king and over time Saul became prideful and disobedient so God rejected him. In the midst of Samuel's sorrow, though, God comes to him and gives him some instructions. The same message God spoke to Samuel is the same message that He is speaking to all of us, "Let go! It is time to move on! Your loved one may no longer be here, but cherish the memories and live the life I have purposed for you. They may look good to you, but that is not who I told you to choose. Your family may not see the value in you, but I do. Yes, they hurt you, lied on you, slept with you without loving you, and even betrayed you, but it is time for you to freefall into a new place in ME." What do you need to let go of: a person, a relationship, a painful situation, past hurt, bitterness, pride, low self-esteem, disappointment, envy, anger, jealousy, haughtiness? You have mourned long enough. Release it, and ask God to replace it with joy, hope, peace, love, confidence, and humility. Take some time out and ask Him to give you a new perspective and some instructions on what you should do. Ask him to give you the courage to walk away. Pray for strength to forgive. Take some time daily to meditate upon his promises and know that he is not a respecter of persons. Stop living in the past when you have the present and a hope for tomorrow. After I made a conscious decision to let go, after I did the freefall, we pulled the cord, and I was lifted up to higher heights when the parachute opened. While I am not advising everyone to go and enroll in skydiving classes, I am challenging you to liberate yourself from all the things that you know are keeping you from living FREE. Do not mourn too long. Take risks. Let go. Break the limitations. There are new levels you have yet to conquer. Live Free or Die Hard.

Prayer: Father, thank you for giving us life on purpose. Give us the boldness and the courage to let go of the things that hinder us, and help us to heed your voice in every decision we make. We proclaim liberty. In Jesus name I pray, Amen.

WHAT YOU CAN DO TO CHANGE THE WORLD

Luke 4:18 KJV

The Spirit of the Lord is upon me, because he hath anointed me to preach the gospel to the poor; he hath sent me to heal the brokenhearted, to preach deliverance to the captives, and recovering of sight to the blind, to set at liberty them that are bruised.

Matthew 28:19-20 KJV

Go ye therefore, and teach all nations, baptizing them in the name of the Father, and of the Son, and of the Holy Ghost: (20) Teaching them to observe all things whatsoever I have commanded you: and, lo, I am with you always, {even} unto the end of the world. Amen.

John 14:12

I tell you the truth, anyone who has faith in me will do what I have been doing. He will do even greater things than these, because I am going to the Father.

What Would You Do?

◆　◆　◆　◆　◆　◆　◆　◆　◆　◆　◆　◆　◆　◆　◆　◆

"Let each of you esteem and look upon and be concerned for not his own interests, but also each for the interests of others. Let this same attitude and purpose and mind be in you which was in Christ Jesus."

Philippians 2:4-5

As I was on my way to the Main Post Office in Dallas, there was a man at the traffic light with a sign that read, "Why Lie - - Beer". Just last week there were a couple sistas selling M&Ms and Pixie Sticks at a traffic light. Jehovah Witnesses pound the pavement daily in order to spread their message. Muslims stand firm and will die for their beliefs. Think about that for a minute. The beggar wants something so desperately that he is willing to be humiliated and talked about to get it. The sistas need a little pocket change, so there is no shame in their game. The Witnesses get doors slammed in their faces; they get ridiculed, and yet they get up every morning and continue to spread their message. And for the sake of religion, Muslims willingly die. Now what would you do? Are you so hungry and desperate for God that you would wear a sign that reads, "Hungry - Will Worship for God"? Would you be willing to go buy groceries for the family who does not have any food (without telling anyone you did it)? Would you be willing to walk several miles to find that lost person in the midst of rejection and poor weather conditions? Would you die in the name of our Lord Jesus? Are you willing to help others without ever receiving a thank you? Well friends, your answers should all be "Yes!" We say we're Christ followers. We say we want to be like Jesus. We say we want to do what he did. He showed others how to get better...He did not talk about them and judge them. He took all a little boy had and showed the people that through prayer and faith, their little could become much. He walked and talked and loved and shared in spite of mockery and haters and persecution. And most of all, He gave his life. He died for you, and He died for me. What are you going to do?

Prayer: Father, we are going to do whatever it takes to let our attitudes be the same as that of Christ Jesus. Show us how to befriend the prodigal sons and daughters, those who are dealing with depression and loneliness and low self-esteem and any addictions, and those who may be following a doctrine that is leading them to hell. Use us to change the world. This I ask in the name of Jesus, Amen.

WHAT TO DO WHEN YOU NEED CONFIDENCE

Philippians 4:13

I can do everything through him who gives me strength.

Isaiah 40:31 KJV

But they that wait upon the Lord shall renew their strength; they shall mount up with wings as eagles; they shall run, and not be weary; and they shall walk, and not faint.

John 14:12

I tell you the truth, anyone who has faith in me will do what I have been doing. He will do even greater things than these, because I am going to the Father.

Did I Do That?

◆ ◆ ◆ ◆ ◆ ◆ ◆ ◆ ◆ ◆ ◆ ◆ ◆ ◆ ◆

"I can do everything through him who gives me strength." Philippians 4:13

Steve Urkel was notorious for asking the question, "Did I Do That?" Now this question normally came after he had ruined a situation or messed up royally. It was no surprise to him that, YES, he did do that. As I was meditating on this passage, I started to think about Paul and all the things that he did. He went from persecuting Christians to preaching the gospel. He went from cursing God to casting out demons. He went from damnation to destiny. Think about that. He was on his way to do his own thing, and one day the SON showed up, knocked him off his feet, blinded him, converted him, and then used him for HIS glory. As a result we've got 2/3 of the New Testament. What worries, doubts, uncertainties, and fears have taken residence in your life right now? What has God told you to do that you do not feel capable of doing? Whatever the problem, whomever the Goliath, wherever you are being led, just know that Paul's testimony is the truth, the whole truth and nothing but the truth. In Ebonics, Greek, Hebrew and English, everything means everything. Take the new position. Leave a current position. Make the commitment. Enroll in this upcoming semester. Learn to say, "No" and let it be a complete sentence. Take a stand and be different. The day will come when, like Urkel, you will ask, "Did I Do That?" Then, like, Paul, you will be able to say, "Yes, I did that through Him who gives me strength."

Prayer: Father, thank you for giving us supernatural strength. With you we CAN do everything, so we say, "Thank you". Your grace is sufficient in our weakness. Condition us. Develop us. Build us up, Lord, so that we may bring you glory. In Jesus name I pray, Amen.

WHAT TO DO WHEN YOU FEEL DEPRESSED

Psalm 30:5b KJV

Weeping may endure for a night, but joy cometh in the morning.

Psalm 147:3 KJV

He healeth the broken in heart, and bindeth up their wounds.

Isaiah 43:2 KJV

When thou passest through the waters, I {will be} with thee; and through the rivers, they shall not overflow thee: when thou walkest through the fire, thou shalt not be burned; neither shall the flame kindle upon thee.

Have No Fear. God Is Here!

◆ ◆ ◆ ◆ ◆ ◆ ◆ ◆ ◆ ◆ ◆ ◆ ◆ ◆ ◆ ◆

"Elijah was afraid and ran for his life... v9 There he went into a cave and spent the night. And the word of the Lord came to him, "What are you doing here, Elijah?" 1 Kings 19:3

In the movie, "Forrest Gump", little Jenny wanted him to get away from the bullies so she encouraged him to "Run Forrest, Run!" Like Forrest, Elijah was on the run, hiding out in caves from Jezebel. He had just annihilated the prophets of Baal, yet in this passage we find him scared, running from a woman. Don't be scared, Elijah. "What are you doing here?" HERE, not THERE. You missed your shout. God was right there with him in the midst of his fear, in the midst of his discouragement, in the midst of his emotional breakdown. Right now God is asking you, "What are you doing here depressed when I have given you joy that the world cannot take away. What are you doing here worrying when you know that I took nothing and created everything? What are you doing here afraid when I have given you a spirit of power, love and a sound mind?" God's got businesses for you to start. He has a place in ministry reserved just for you. He has got your Boaz and your Esther just waiting on you. Stop hiding out in caves. Stop running from people. Stop running from your problems. Forrest ran for three years, two months, fourteen days and sixteen hours. Do not spend your life running. Do what Elijah did: Rest. Eat. Listen to God. Trust Him. And, move when He tells you to move. Have No Fear. God Is Here!

Prayer: Father, we thank you for your perfect love that casts out fear. I pray for every person who is afraid and running like the wind right now. Let them know that they cannot outrun your love, your grace, or your presence. Bring every person out of the cave of loneliness, of worry, of fear and move us to the places you want us to be. In Jesus name I pray, Amen.

WHAT TO DO WHEN YOU HAVE A PHYSICAL ILLNESS

3 JOHN 1:2 KJV

Beloved, I wish above all things that thou mayest prosper and be in health, even as thy soul prospereth.

Jeremiah 17:14 KJV

Heal me, O Lord, and I shall be healed; save me, and I shall be saved: for thou art my praise.

James 5:14-15 KJV

Is any sick among you? let him call for the elders of the church; and let them pray over him, anointing him with oil in the name of the Lord: (15) And the prayer of faith shall save the sick, and the Lord shall raise him up; and if he have committed sins, they shall be forgiven him.

Fragile: Handle With Care

◆ ◆ ◆ ◆ ◆ ◆ ◆ ◆ ◆ ◆ ◆ ◆ ◆ ◆ ◆ ◆

"Jonathan, son of Saul, had a son who was lame in both feet. He was five years old when the news about Saul and Jonathan came from Jezreel. His nurse picked him up and fled, but as she hurried to leave, he fell and became crippled. His name was Mephibosheth." 2 Samuel 4:4

I will have to admit that I am a bit clumsy. I have dropped my share of "breakables" and even tripped myself up a few times. Many of those things shattered into tiny pieces that I had to carefully sweep up, and I had to make sure that I did not leave any debris that would cause further damage. Now visualize today's scripture. We are not talking about glass or ceramics. A young boy was dropped and left crippled in both feet, because his nurse received disturbing news that led her to make an impulsive decision. Because of her emotional distress, her careless actions caused irrevocable damage. Who or what has dropped you and left you in pieces? Is it death? A broken relationship? A job? Sometimes our loved ones being in PEACE leaves us in PIECES. When life drops you, you have got to pick up the shattered pieces. You can choose to remain fragmented and broken, or you can ask God to take all those places that are bruised and begin the healing process. Ask Him to mend your broken heart and to fill it with his unconditional love. Ask Him to put together a new attitude towards men or women. Ask Him to replace your unstable work history with job security. If you are feeling crippled right now and just want to be like those pieces that are swept away and tossed out, I encourage you to keep on reading to Chapter 9. Mephibosheth's condition did not change who he was, Saul's grandson, and King David sought after him and gave him a permanent place at his table. Like Mephibosheth, your condition does not change who you are - A King's kid, a co-heir with Christ. With every imperfection, your lameness, and all your brokenness, God wants you to sit at His table. Let Him put together the shattered pieces of your broken life. You may be fragile right now, but He Will Handle You With Care!!!

Prayer: Father, in the name of Jesus, I pray healing for every person who is broken and hurting right now. Please heal them emotionally, spiritually and physically in every area that they are hurting. Please remove anyone or anything that is a hindrance more than a help to them. I thank you in advance for wholeness and for handling each and every one of us with care. In Jesus name I pray, Amen.

WHAT TO DO WHEN SEEKING FELLOWSHIP WITH GOD

Revelation 3:20 KJV

Behold, I stand at the door, and knock: if any man hear my voice, and open the door, I will come in to him, and will sup with him, and he with me.

John 15:7 KJV

If ye abide in me, and my words abide in you, ye shall ask what ye will, and it shall be done unto you.

Zechariah 2:10

"Shout and be glad, O Daughter of Zion. For I am coming, and I will live among you," declares the LORD.

Get a Little Closer

◆ ◆ ◆ ◆ ◆ ◆ ◆ ◆ ◆ ◆ ◆ ◆ ◆ ◆ ◆ ◆

"Draw near to God and he will draw near to you..." James 4:8

My sister and I shared a room growing up. We also had to share a bed. I could not touch her. There could be no part of my body on her side, and I had better not pull any of the covers off of her at any point during the night. To this day, I think that is why I sleep on the edge of the bed. It is funny how the not-so-little things that happened in the past affect what we do and how we respond to others today. Maybe you did not fit in growing up, and now you have low self-esteem. Maybe you were always the last one picked for dodge ball or the other fun games, and you now have a fear of rejection. Maybe someone you loved hurt you really bad, and now you will not let anybody else get close to you. How about that girl or guy friend who betrayed your trust, and now you struggle with building relationships with other people? No matter what we have been through in our past; No matter how insecure or how many issues we have, God tells us that he wants a relationship with us just the way we are. Can't you hear Him whispering in your ear, "Get a little closer; don't be shy." You do not have to shave or put on any makeup. Whenever you feel alone, call Him. He will come over. He will comfort you. You can talk and laugh or just spend some quiet time in one another's presence. And when it gets late, or you get restless, He says, "Slide on over here to my side. You can touch me." He will wrap his loving arms around you. You will share some "pillow talk". Draw close to God and allow Him to show you how to tear down your walls so that other people can slide in and get next to you.

Prayer: Father, we thank you for your omnipresence. Forgive us for all the times we thought we were all alone. You were with us the whole time. Teach us how to trust you, even when we do not feel you near. In the good times and in the bad times, Lord, I pray that each of us draws near to you. Give us boldness as we come before you and woo us with your promises and your love. In Jesus name I pray, Amen.

WHAT TO DO WHEN YOU ARE WAITING ON GOD

Isaiah 40:31 KJV

But they that wait upon the Lord shall renew their strength; they shall mount up with wings as eagles; they shall run, and not be weary; {and} they shall walk, and not faint.

Habakkuk 2:3 KJV

For the vision is yet for an appointed time, but at the end it shall speak, and not lie: though it tarry, wait for it; because it will surely come, it will not tarry.

Psalm 27:14 KJV

Wait on the Lord: be of good courage, and he shall strengthen thine heart: wait, I say, on the Lord.

Expect Delays

◆ ◆ ◆ ◆ ◆ ◆ ◆ ◆ ◆ ◆ ◆ ◆ ◆ ◆ ◆ ◆

Joshua 3:2 "After three days, the officers went throughout the camp," (NIV)

Have you ever seen those flashing electronic signs on the highway that say, "Expect Delays?" You appreciate the advance warning, but when you have places to go and people to see, you do not want anything to get in your way. An accident. Bad weather. A family emergency. Traffic. A heavy workload. These are some of the things that can delay us from getting to where we need to be in a timely manner. But think about the Israelites and their situation. Those three days of waiting at the Jordan River were days of preparation for crossing it. They had waited 40 years, so what was three more days? As they waited, no doubt some of them were saying, "Man, we should go back!" Some were probably saying, "Hey, it looks pretty good on this side of the river to me." They did not have time to build a bridge. They would not have made it across by swimming. Not by their might, not by their power, but by His spirit, so they waited. The leaders had to show courage in the face of danger. They had to build up the people's faith by redirecting the focus away from "the impossible" toward the greatness of God. So what can we learn from today's verse: Our faith will require us to wait. Wait means to remain or wait in expectation. Trust God while you are at the edge of your Jordan. He does not need you to figure out what He has already worked out. You are going somewhere. He is navigating your path. You may be delayed but not denied.

Prayer: Father, thank you for expectancy. While we wait, I pray that you give us complete faith in you. Help us to be cautious and to make keen decisions before making irrational decisions. As we prepare to cross over into our destiny, attune our ears to hear from you, because we trust you. In Jesus name I pray, Amen.

WHAT TO DO WHEN YOU NEED GUIDANCE

John 10:27-28 KJV

My sheep hear my voice, and I know them, and they follow me: (28) And I give unto them eternal life; and they shall never perish, neither shall any man pluck them out of my hand.

Psalm 119:105 KJV

Thy word is a lamp unto my feet, and a light unto my path.

Psalm 23:6 KJV

Surely goodness and mercy shall follow me all the days of my life: and I will dwell in the house of the Lord forever.

Get To Steppin'

◆ ◆ ◆ ◆ ◆ ◆ ◆ ◆ ◆ ◆ ◆ ◆ ◆ ◆ ◆ ◆

"The steps of a good man are ordered by the Lord: and he delighteth in his way." Psalm 37:23

It is always exciting to see babies take their first steps. We have all been there. Think about it. For months you are crawling around and having to depend upon someone else to get you where you need to go. The walker was supposed to be a reward to help you move about freely, but it ended up being a hindrance, because it was big and just got in the way. And now think about those times when you saw the toddler trying to pull himself up to something stable, something that he could hold on to. Even when babies fall, they get back up and try again. Without directions and without any pressure, they learn to take one step at a time. Sometimes they get excited and get a little ahead of themselves, but to see the joy and their Kool-Aid grin is all worth it. Aren't we just like those babies? No matter how old we are or how independent we try to be, we need God to lead and guide us in every decision we make and in every word we speak. Our solid foundation is His Word, and He tells us that He orders our steps in His word. If we grab hold and hang on to every promise He has made, this solid rock will never let us down. Do not allow other people to lead you the wrong way. Do not let them influence you to go back to crawling. God will order your steps. He will not confine you to a walker but will give you the ability to move about freely, and He will take away the obstacles that are in your way. Sometimes it takes a fall before we learn to appreciate all the steps that got us to the place we are now. Take one step at a time. Take one book of the Bible at a time. Take one memory verse at a time. Whatever it takes, Get To Steppin'.

Prayer: Father, thank you for ordering our steps in your Word. Sometimes we do not know where to go or how to get there, so Holy Spirit I ask that you give us clear directions and guidance. We want to step, Lord, but we need you to keep us on the right path. In Jesus name I pray, Amen.

WHAT TO DO WHEN YOU NEED TO FEEL ACCEPTED

1 Samuel 16:7

But the Lord said to Samuel, "Do not look on his appearance or on the height of his stature, because I have rejected him. For the Lord sees not as man sees: man looks on the outward appearance, but the Lord looks on the heart.

Psalm 27:10

When my father and my mother forsake me, then the Lord will take me up.

Psalm 139:14

I praise you, for I am fearfully and wonderfully made. Wonderful are your works; that I know very well.

America's Next Top Model

◆ ◆ ◆ ◆ ◆ ◆ ◆ ◆ ◆ ◆ ◆ ◆ ◆ ◆ ◆ ◆

Matt. 7:1 "Do not judge, or you too will be judged."

One of the hottest shows on TV is "America's Next Top Model". The premise of the show is a group of supermodel wannabes who come together and compete for a modeling contract and extra rewards. Each week they are given new challenges, and then the contestants have to face the judges. They get critiqued on how well they handled the challenges, their appearance and mannerisms...anything the judges choose to talk to them about. At the end of each episode, the person who does not live up to the judge's standards is eliminated. Think about that for a moment. Is that not what happens to us everyday? You might be the model wannabe who is striving to win the challenges that come your way and remain humble. You may be the one who is not the most talented or the most beautiful, but you have a good heart and kind spirit. You may even be trying to exemplify model behavior by studying the Word, praying more, and serving in ministry, yet, people still talk about you. But which side are you on? Are you sitting on the judge's panel? Are you talking about other people's issues instead of praying them through? How many people have you eliminated, because they did not look a certain way? Maybe you judge your brothers or sisters who fall into sexual sin as they make their way down this Christian Catwalk. The scripture tells us not to judge, or we too, will be judged. We have all got issues. We all have flaws and imperfections. One day we will all end up going before the Judge, and what an honor to be crowned "The Kingdom's Top Model", because we lived according to His standards.

Prayer: Jesus, thank you for exemplifying model behavior while you were here on earth. Thank you for showing us how to love and have compassion on those who do not think or dress or act like us. Continue to teach us the importance of accepting people for who they are and help them to live up to your standards, not ours. In Jesus name I pray, Amen.